YOUR KNOWLEDGE HAS

Bibliographic information published by the German National Library:

The German National Library lists this publication in the National Bibliography;
detailed bibliographic data are available on the Internet at http://dnb.dnb.de .

Imprint:

Copyright © 2009 GRIN Verlag, Open Publishing GmbH
Print and binding: Books on Demand GmbH, Norderstedt Germany
ISBN: 9783640974313

This book at GRIN:

http://www.grin.com/en/e-book/176307/english-hooliganism-a-different-social-
movement

Anonym

Aus der Reihe: e-fellows.net stipendiaten-wissen

e-fellows.net (Hrsg.)

Band 153

English Hooliganism - A Different Social Movement

GRIN Publishing

GRIN - Your knowledge has value

Since its foundation in 1998, GRIN has specialized in publishing academic texts by students, college teachers and other academics as e-book and printed book. The website www.grin.com is an ideal platform for presenting term papers, final papers, scientific essays, dissertations and specialist books.

Visit us on the internet:

http://www.grin.com/

http://www.facebook.com/grincom

http://www.twitter.com/grin_com

English Hooliganism - A "Different" Social Movement

Research Paper

Course: Social Movements and Political Participation

Jacobs University Bremen

Spring 2009

I. Introduction

More than 37 million spectators attended football games in 2007-08 while 3,842 people were arrested for disorder connected to matches according to the UK Home Office. Of those arrests, 373 were for violent crimes – an increase of 33 over the previous season. On the other hand, 67% of matches were problem-free and did not result in any arrest. Instead, 60% of football-related arrests took place outside or away from the football stadia (Home Office, 2008). These statistics show that football violence is at least remarkable enough to draw attention of government departments and statisticians. In the past decades, numerous scholars have tried to analyse the roots and dynamics of this violent fan behaviour (Dunning, 2000) that has been labelled 'Hooliganism'. The name-giving implies that football-related violence is considered as more than just some weekly disturbances. It is regarded as a social phenomenon which needs to be observed, investigated, and defined which can eventually lead to an understanding of and response to this behaviour. In our paper we will expose to what extent this phenomenon can be classified as a social movement. Before, we will look at the rise and growth of Hooliganism exemplifying it with some extreme occurrences. We are going to describe Hooligan behaviour and the people who engage in it trying to pin point typical characteristics and motivations of Hooligans. Doing that we want to justify that Hooliganism can be understood as a social movement which will allow us to apply different social movement models on Hooliganism. In order to arrive at the rationale of Hooliganism a descriptive definition is necessary which will give the further analyses and interpretation a basic framework. With several similar definitions of Hooliganism to choose from, the one meaning that we are going to use as a point of departure terms Hooliganism as "competitive violence of socially organized fan groups in football, principally directed against opposing fan groups" (Spaaij, 2006, p. 11).

II. History of English Hooliganism: Rise and Growth

Even though the denoting term 'Hooliganism' was not born, yet, football violence accompanied the sport in England from the beginning throughout almost all of its existence. Having a closer look at only the 20th century, complaints about "noise, swearing and rowdiness" (Armstrong, 1998, p. 6) were reported first in the 1920s and 1930s. However, it was only after the Second World War when the phenomenon really started to take off. Several explanations might help to understand why at this particular time the old-fashioned and well-recognized English 'fair-play' behaviour, which included the fan groups, gradually vanished. Armstrong (1998) and Brimson (2000) argue that this coincided with the end of English national military service in the 1960s, which altered young men's horizon dramatically. Now the match-going took over the aura of a credibility test and masculinity would be

1

proved in the context of football. It is also in that time when the term 'Hooligan' became publicly known. As a side note, this is etymologically speaking quite unrelated as it stems most probably from stories about an immigrant Irish family with the surname 'Houlihan', terrorizing East London in the 19th century (Brimson, 2000, p. 81). In the 1962 World Cup in Chile, English fans saw how fan groups of other countries engaged in a much more intense and violent behaviour which again gave the domestic Hooliganism vital momentum. Generally, the development was supported by a new generation that opposed obedience vis-à-vis the authorities, fought against hierarchies and aimed at curtailing the power of the state. In the realm discussed here, it meant of course challenging and fighting the police present at the stadia.

Hooligans in England continued to expand in terms of activists, violence, and destructive behaviour throughout the 1970s. The authorities, powerless and barely able to react, failed in embanking the movement. Hooligans refined their methods, for instance in how to best smuggle objects into the stadia, 'construct' weapons out of newspapers inside the stadium, or they (ab)used missiles to attack opponent fan groups (Brimson, 2000).

Gradually, wide-scale violence exacerbated (Pearson, 2009) even more, making it appropriate to label the 1980s the 'dark' decade for football. Gardner (1996) argues that this is, amongst others, due to the increased violence on the pitch, with brutal fouls on a much more regular basis than today. Illegal destructive and violent Hooligan behaviour took place in such a large and anonymizing mass that even if a criminal action was spotted by the police (difficult enough given the sea of bodies to be found on most terraces), getting the guy out and arrested without retaliation from fellow fans was incredibly difficult. Similar problems arose from the arrival of the "Casual" scene. This meant that Hooligans began to dress in expensive clothes, unrelated to a specific football club making them unidentifiable for the police beforehand. After several incidents with singular persons being killed out of Hooligan violence, 1985 saw the first great football-fan-related catastrophe: at the Bradford City Fire disaster, 56 people lost their lives when a flash fire destroyed one side of Bradford's football stadium. Whereas this was not caused by violent fan behaviour, only a few months later Liverpool Hooligans were indeed mainly responsible for fan attacks and a resulting terrible crush at the European Cup Final in Belgium (Brimson, 2000). The "Heysel Disaster" causing 39 casualties amongst the visitors has arguably been the worst case of football Hooliganism in Europe until today. English Hooligans hit the headlines of every newspaper, and the public demand for finally tackling this movement could not be overheard anymore. However, the authorities, still not capable to genuinely understand the scope of the Hooligan development and momentum, introduced policies that qualify best as cosmetic changes, if at all. The "Sporting Event Act" of 1985 for example, despite its bulky name, merely forbad drunken fans to enter a stadium (Armstrong, 1998). Also, huge metal fences were erected to separate and cage the two groups. "English soccer stadiums began to resemble concentration camps" (Gardner, 1996, p. 202). Eventually, at Hillsborough in 1989, this described similarity turned into deadly serious reality. For a FA-Cup game between Liverpool and Nottingham, fans tried to get in an overcrowded stadium that was already bursting. The police, heavily criticized in the aftermath, opened an additional gate with the intention to relieve the pressure on the tribunes. In contrast, even more fans put pressure onto the fenced-in tribunes from outside. In this massive crush, 96 people were killed. It was "the event that changed everything" (Brimson, 2000, p. 128), and it had a long-lasting impact – also and especially on the English Hooligan movement.

Prime Minister Margret Thatcher herself called for immediate action. Lord Taylor of Gosforth headed the investigations and presented in his report 78 measures on how to prevent such catastrophes in the future (Pentz & Köster, n.d.). This "Taylor Report" on the one hand put pressure on the clubs to bring their own house in order through major infrastructural changes. This was put into practice for instance with the most visible difference that every English stadium had to become all-seater with no more standing areas. In addition, the authorities demanded more security, which resulted in an increasing number of private stewards in the stadia and CCTV camera set-ups. Moreover, the corralling metal fences had to be removed. On the other hand, destructive fan behaviour and Hooliganism were directly tackled. In order to introduce more diversity and calm groups to the games, football clubs sought to attract families and women. Certain clubs promoted for instance discounted Family Tickets. Contrarily, clubs intended to dispose of the 'troublemakers' from the lower classes attending the games and being considered as the main source for Hooliganism. Consequently, seasonal tickets prices jumped up by 300% within one year or were only available through costly special membership status (Brown, 1998). This "Pricing Out" was thought to support a more civilized atmosphere in the stadium (Armstrong, 1998, p. 124-132) and also strengthened the business character of the clubs. Manchester United made this commercialization particularly recognizable by changing the official name from FC (Football Club) to PLC (Public Limited Company), entering the stock market and attracting investors with the intention to reach a new customer base (Brown, 1998).

Paralyzed from the past incidents and hit by those new policies, Hooliganism kept quiet for the beginning of the 1990s. Above all, the stadia themselves were no longer a dangerous place for the normal spectator whose safety really increased. Yet, as Pearson (2009) rightly points out: Hooliganism changed, it did not decline. We would thus describe that development stage as 'Hooligans going backstage'. Profiting for example from the upcoming mobile phone for coordination (Brimson, 2000), Hooligans moved their actions away from the actual football grounds where their behaviour was no longer tolerated. Instead, opponent groups clashed at train stations, in the city centre, or even at remote places which were communicated through phone calls (Armstrong, 1998). No matter if the battles were scheduled beforehand or spontaneous, they occurred at places and at times unexpected for the police and hence, could live on up until today.

The generally improved situation in the English top leagues nowadays has also led to a loosening of the tight regulations and surveillance that existed in the 1990s. Above all, England was of course frightened of an explosion of Hooliganism when hosting the Eurocup 1996. As this event went without major disturbances, despite severe media instigations (Brimson, 2000), afterwards Hooligans, especially of the lower amateur league clubs, have benefited from renewed liberties in recent years. The internet and new media tools allow for an even better coordination of 'backstage' Hooligan action. In conclusion, only the fact that the movement is no longer on the front cover of the print press destroying the stadia does not mean it has lost its momentum. Hooligans have adapted to new regulations, they have learned how to circumvent the authorities – and they are certainly not in decline.

III. Characterizing the Movement

Right at the beginning it should be emphasized that the movement of Hooliganism, and more precisely its members, are a highly diverse group. All major publications agree that, from the unemployed low class worker to the London City investment banker, basically all societal groups are represented. Having this acknowledged, our simplified approach of characterizing Hooliganism is by exploring the "stereotypical" Hooligan, representing the major share of the movement, in particular the persons engaging in the most violent forms.

Field Research as well as quantitative evidence (Armstrong, 1998; Brimson, 2000; Buford, 1991; Dunning, 2000; Spaaij, 2006) manifests that this type of Hooligan is usually male, young, and single. He has a low education, but he is by no means excluded from society. This person is employed and, thus, can be classified in the lower working class. Dunning (2000) proves empirically this class belonging by compiling data from various studies, which all find that the majority of Hooligans stem from the working classes. The average Hooligan has also come to the attention of the criminal justice system, though only for minor delinquencies; so this is not about felons that spent several years in prison. A crucial element is of course that an intrinsic conviction prevails that the football contest should not be confined to the pitch. As Wagner (2002, p. 34) illustrates, many Hooligans impatiently wait for the game to end in order to start the "third half" outside of the stadium. Furthermore, alcohol plays an important role for Hooligans, obviously far beyond a sensible level. In addition, muscular torsos and tattoos are often "desirable" (Armstrong, 1998, p. 162) for a masculine appearance, whereas any homosexual leanings would consequently lead to an exclusion of the Hooligan movement. This goes well together with the widely outlined importance for the man to strive for credible masculinity and respect from his peers. What Brimson (2000) calls "Buzz", or Armstrong (1998) labels "aggressive excitement", it points at this thrill, which Hooligans experience in their group when they engage in violent actions and, consequently, acquire peer respect by taking those risks. It is the central feature which, in addition to the shared identities of the group members and ardent support for the respective English football club, ties the Hooligan group together and contributes to the keeps the movement's persistence.

Examining now the movement on the group-level, one can also depict general features that the "firms", as the English Hooligan groups are also called, have in common. The organizational structure is very egalitarian, consensus-oriented and a rather unorganized than organized collectivity. Armstrong (1998) describes, based on various examples, how a "firm" continuously argues over which actions to take or even which pub to go to before the game. This makes it obvious that there is no formal leader. Singular persons might organize the coach for an away game, but such responsibilities are neither officially stated nor in any way reliable for a longer period of time. One cannot observe a certain body within the Hooligan group that would qualify as senior leadership. Hence, the whole mass is quite anonymous (Brimson, 2000), with mere acquaintanceship level among its members. Basically, everyone is welcome who has free time, money at hand, and the willingness to fight for the 'right' cause, i.e. the respective football club. Consequently, the community is characterized by vague and unstable boundaries, as every member can also leave at any point of time. Thus too, a limited degree of trust within the "firm" is observable. One would help the fellow fan who is attacked by the opponents, but there is always an underlying degree of mistrustfulness, since unknown members could also be intruders from either the police or a rivalry fan groups (Armstrong, 1998).

Bearing in mind the listed characteristics of the Hooligan movement, one may rightly classify them as a clique, according to Boissevain (1974, p. 174): "A coalition whose members associate regularly with each other on the basis of affection and common interest and possess a sense of common identity." In summary, this relatively low degree of integration in a "firm" can be seen as its actual strength, because this makes it so hard for the police to know who actually takes part, what the Hooligans have planned, to pinpoint responsibilities and, generally, to successfully fight the movement.

5

IV. A Theoretical Understanding of Hooliganism

Although the descriptive approach towards Hooliganism may be quite unequivocal, figuring out the core of this social problem seems to be more ambiguous as numerous scholars from different academic fields such as anthropology, psychology, and sociology differ in their understandings of Hooliganism (Armstrong, 1998; Dunning, 2000; Kerr, 1994). Unlike other social movements that have a clear mission or aim to change their social or political environment, Hooligans with their disruptive behaviour appear to have no purpose or deliberate goal at all. This is why Hooliganism may not be considered as a social movement at first sight. However, in order to indeed relate Hooliganism to the social movement models it is essential to look at these various perceptions of the motivations of fan aggression. For that, an overview of the most prominent theoretical explanations will be provided as follows. It is particularly remarkable that some scientists theorize Hooliganism by placing a deeper meaning in the violent behaviour of the supporters, whereas other scholars see those interpretations as exaggerations of a behavioural pattern that can be explained in a much simpler manner by merely looking at human nature.

Anthropological Approach

Belonging to the latter group and basing their line of argumentation on comprehensive in-depth analysis of the Hooligans in Sheffield (England), Armstrong and Harris (1991) represent the Anthropological Approach. They mainly argue that football violence is not at all organized but rather an expression of male identity rituals. With their contentious behaviour Hooligans tend to seek some kind of accomplishment in a group that consists of diverse members but with common ideals and thus developing a shared identity and sense of belonging (Armstrong, 1998).

Furthermore, they accuse the police and media for falsely claiming that Hooligan violence is a product of deliberate group structures that are even built in hierarchies. These conspiratorial allegations result from the shortcomings of both the media and police in how to cope with, classify, or encounter Hooliganism (Ibid.). It would make intuitive sense to confirm that this provocative behaviour is a means of creating bondages between the Hooligan group members. By having this common goal to not only have their team win against the other team, but even more importantly to triumph over the other team's supporters and show them that they are stronger, they grow together. It is this feeling of 'us' versus 'them' giving the members strength that Armstrong (1998) emphasizes and that supports the perspective of regarding Hooliganism as a collective action which again is not far from being classified as a social movement (Braun & Vliegenthart, 2008).

Even though this approach has been criticized for underestimating the gravity of the violence and generalizing behavioural motivations by relying on individual testimonies of only one club, it shall still be highly valuable for our attempt of linking Hooliganism to models of social movements. The qualitative data provided by the author should not be ignored as it actually reflects the personal motivations of fans in the Hooligan scene.

Psychological Approach

Another theory which does not differ so severely from the anthropological one is Kerr's (1994) Psychological Reversal Theory. Here, it is argued that Hooligans seek to escape from their boring every-day life by engaging in violent delinquencies deviating from social norms in the football environment (Kerr, 1994).

Kerr explains that the Hooligans' confrontations with the police as much as with other Hooligan groups, and the attention of the media generates a feeling of arousal and excitement in them. This 'acting against the norm', breaking the rules and engaging in destruction stimulate their need to change their emotional state from boredom to their adventurous 'kick of the week' (Ibid.). Kerr is criticized for neglecting the significance of the role of masculinity having a great impact on the motivations of Hooligans (Dunning, 2000). Moreover, Dunning is not impressed by Kerr's reasoning regarding the need to change the 'boredom' state which he sees to be not sufficient to explain the quest for excitement (Ibid.). Claiming that he developed a similar but much more comprehensive interpretation years before Kerr, Dunning values 'routinisation' rather than 'boredom' as the motivation for the adventure of violent actions (Elias & Dunning, 1986).

Sharing Kerr's view, Finn (1994) goes even beyond the aspect of emotional arousal of the individual. He emphasizes the Hooligans' quest for 'flow' or 'peak' emotions that are experienced in a collective, and thus enforce the common group identity (Finn, 1994). It would be reasonable here to refer to Zimbardo's deindividuation and the psychology of mobs (1970). Although he does not specialize in Hooligan groups his theories about certain dynamics in large groups are very relevant in this context. Zimbardo (1970) states that people in groups give up some sense of responsibility or assessment of their current situation. This lowers their threshold to engage in impulsive and radical activities which they would usually avoid when acting as an individual. That applied to Hooligan groups would lead to the understanding that Hooligans are more susceptible to violent actions in their Hooligan groups. This is because these actions are taken in a collective and the members will not be held liable individually for the consequences. Also, in these groups it is easier to generate this emotional arousal as the members can push each other developing collective dynamics.

Marxist Approach

Before the publication of these psychological view-points, sociologists have already tried to arrive at the causes of Hooliganism, one of the pioneers being Ian Taylor (1987). With what is later called the Marxist Approach (Frosdick & Marsh, 2005) he explains the emergence of fan aggression through the "embourgeoisement of football" (Taylor , 1971, p. 372).

Owing to the increasing popularity of football worldwide the various clubs became more organized and thus commercialized. Consequently, football was not merely a game any longer but developed into a profitable industry that was run by entrepreneurs. The players received higher, if not even tremendous salaries and attained celebrity status. All this alienated the majority of the working-class football fans who felt excluded from this mainstream approach to the game of football and lost their connection to their local clubs. Therefore their involvement in Hooligan activities can be interpreted as a "working-class resistance movement" which is driven by the desire of regaining control over their favourite sport (Ibid.). Although all this may sound very plausible and generate some empathy for the Hooligans who were supposedly suppressed by the football elites, the theory lacks empirical data and is not in accordance with the testimonies of Hooliganism.

Figurational Approach

Dunning and his colleagues from the Leicester School have so far collected most of the significant empirical data related to Hooligans and are mostly referred to by non-English scholars that are concerned with the topic (Frosdick & Marsh, 2005). In their Figurational Approach they seem to unify some aspects of the psychological approach and the working-class element of the Marxist standpoint. Just as Kerr, they understand Hooligan behaviour to be driven by the Hooligans' quest to feel emotionally aroused (Dunning, 2000).

However, they look at a bigger picture and see more than male adolescents fighting each other to get a kick out of it. As mentioned in earlier sections of the paper, their statistically significant analyses show that Hooligan groups in England predominantly comprise of working classes – not neglecting that Hooligans with higher social status are at least present (Ibid.) This finding would correspond to Taylor's (1987) focus on the lower social strata. But the Leicester School scholars do not see the fan violence as some kind of movement against the football elites in order to fight the commercialization of the game. Basing their hypotheses on a wide array of personal statements by Hooligans, they conclude that next to the pursuit of excitement, also masculinity and physical strength play a crucial role. As these Hooligans with their working-class backgrounds do not enjoy any prestige or power in their 'normal' lives, it is the football environment, where they earn respect and acknowledgment among the Hooligan members (Dunning et al., 1988). Displaying their virile capabilities they acquire the meaning and status that they usually lack.

Furthermore, it is noted that members of the working-classes are more susceptible to engaging into violent behaviour as in their rough working-class environment such behaviour is more salient and tolerated if not even rewarded (Dunning et al., 1988).

Being criticized for their theory only being applicable to the social strata discrepancies typical for England, Dunning admits their initial generalization and hypothesizes that Hooliganism in general may be "fuelled and contoured" by the major "fault lines" of particular countries (Dunning, 2000, p. 141). This, however, remains a mere hypothesis and is suggested to be further investigated on an empirical level (Ibid.).

These were the most renowned approaches towards theorizing Hooliganism – many more could be mentioned as research in this field seems to be inflationary. Not including the Postmodernist Approach advocated by Redhead and Giulianotti in this paper is done deliberately. Their foci are the new generations of Hooligans that represent a clear break from the older and violent forms of football fandom by turning the sensationalized fan image into a friendly one (Frosdick & Marsh, 2005). They can, however, only be observed in specific Hooligan groups in Scotland and Denmark and are thus not relevant for us and our topic of particularly 'English' Hooliganism.

In the end, the extremely comprehensive amount of research that has been undertaken only shows how intransparent Hooligan behaviour and the people engaging in it are. Despite the different interpretations of the roots and motivations of fan aggression, it can be clearly agreed on that Hooligan acts are done in a collective. Social movements are also emphasized to be collective actions that do not necessarily have to pursue a political or social change. In these movements a group consciousness is developed that generates a sense of belonging within the individual member and solidarity among the members (Heberle, 1968). Confirming that Hooliganism can in fact be seen as the 'other' social movement, it is now time to find out what kind of social movement we are dealing with.

V. Hooliganism and Social Movement Models – A Successful Match?

This paper so far has argued that English Hooliganism is a social movement and explained why it is indeed suitable to consider it as such. In this section, four selected prominent academic Models of social movements serve as empirical tools to investigate whether Hooliganism really falls into a broader pattern of social movements, which would strengthen our hypothesis. If Hooliganism is to be characterized as a social movement, it should have a successful match with at least one of the Models presented. For this purpose, Models from various temporal periods and backgrounds are chosen, namely the "Classical", "Political", "Cultural", and "Defiance" Model. Furthermore, by applying the English Hooliganism movement to the respective Models, their strengths, but also deficiencies will be clearly identified. Hence, this real-world example will also assist to further the assessment of the overall performance and usefulness of the competing Models by testing their applicability to a modern and unusual movement.

The first framework to be looked at is the "Classical Model" conceptualized by Parsons (1965) with references to Durkheim (1893, 1897), Weber (1946), and Tönnies (1957). Being starkly influenced by the historical contexts such as the rise of the workers' movement in the 19th century, communism and then fascism, social movements are here seen as irrational collective behaviour that deviates from the social norms and harms social order. Although the violent behaviour of Hooligans can hardly be compared to the actions of the Nazis or Communists, it can indeed be said that Hooligans act rather irrationally with the impulse leading them to destruction and violence which would confirm a match with the "Classical Model" – they even mention mob violence.

Moreover, the Model sees the emergence of social movements to be rooted in the rise of mass society caused by the decline of community (Greer, 1958) in which the individual becomes more and more isolated. This deficiency of societal inclusion induces the desire to find new bondages and new forms of attachment (Heberle, 1968). This corresponds to Hooliganism in that sense that many members, particularly the young male adolescents, find a sense of belonging and group identity in the Hooligan scene. The "Classical Model" would also support our standpoint that Hooligans want to escape their constrained everyday routine by losing themselves in these larger groups where they can diffuse responsibility – as referred to in the psychology of mobs – and just deliberate themselves from their overly rationalized lives.

Another match can be found in how members are characterized in the "Classical Model". Due to their alienation from society (which could be referred to Taylor's alienated fans) they tend to be more susceptible to engage in deviant behaviour that is steered by strong group dynamics. They are in need of strong attachments and are drawn by groups that can grant them a sense of membership. The criterion that is only partially fulfilled by Hooliganism is how the "Classical Model" predicts the decline of social movements, namely by certain rather repressive measures by the authorities. As mentioned, fan violence within the stadia has decreased since the introduction of mandatory all-seater stadia, higher security levels, and the police's harsh courses of action against aggressive fans. However, as Hooliganism *per se* did not vanish but rather changed its venue to off-stadia locations, these adjustments done in the top-down approach were successful only to a certain degree.

Also, looking at the form of social movement Hooliganism would lean towards the "Classical Model" which views movements as disorganized and chaotic. We perceive Hooligan groups as not organized to a certain extent. Some fights evolve out of the situation without any action plan whereas other clashes between different club supporters are arranged battles that are set up in an egalitarian and non-hierarchical manner and taking place in an off-stadium area. So it can indeed be seen as partially organized while the chaotic attribute would rather refer to the absence of a leader in the Hooligan scene. Since the Hooligan groups are very much consensus-based collectives, we would have to reject the leaders such as populists, charlatans and manipulative authorities suggested by the "Classical Model". Another incongruity with this Model is its duration of the social movement. It understands social movements to not last long as they will be encountered by authorities whereas Hooliganism is not on the decline looking back at its long history and cannot be considered as temporary.

The next step will be applying the "Political Model", advocated by McAdam (1982), Tarrow (1994) and Kriesi, Willem & Giugni 1995), to (English) Hooliganism. As the name already implies in this Model politics play a crucial role. Exemplifying the American Civil Rights Movement, labour unions, professionalized movements and so-called 'Not-In-My-Backyard'-groups (NIMBY) the Model puts social movements into the role of aiming at changing the political or social environment to the positive. This is already inconsistent with English Hooliganism as we really cannot understand the Hooligan aggression as a means to accomplish any kind of major societal transformations.

None of the social movements criteria employed by the Political Modal are in accordance with Hooliganism. The Political Model sees the cause and emergence of social movements in the members' perceptions that there will always be conflicts and cannot be avoided. What fluctuates are the openings in the political systems as well the availably of resources and mobilization of people. This cannot be related to Hooligans at all, as Hooligans are simply not politically motivated to participate in collective actions. Their collective action is not driven by interests in specific societal issues. Neither are Hooligan groups headed by business-oriented leaders who are well-educated and financially well-situated as manifested in the Political Model.

The only match that can be determined between Hooliganism and the Political Model is in the duration of the social movement. The Political Model predicts a long or at least recurring live for the social movement and Hooliganism is, as already proven, a movement with a long history that has yet to decline. However, this shared element can hardly suffice to classify Hooliganism in the Political Model.

The third model discussed in depth is based on academic theories *inter alia* by Marcuse (1964), Long (1999) and Touraine (1971). This "Cultural Model" offers interesting basic approaches for a better understanding for example of the student protest movements from the 1960s. Yet, when comparing its central hypothesis with the Hooligan movement, only little accordance can be found. For the explanation of the growth of Hooliganism, we cannot agree with the "Cultural Model", since we reject a priori the idea that the movement developed due to uprising severe (societal) problems. It is to note though that the argument of opening societal fault lines is in alignment with the Figurational Approach (Frosdick & Marsh, 2005) that was introduced in the precedent chapter. On the other hand, as this is still only one out of many theories for explaining Hooligans, this part also does not make the "Cultural Model", much more convincing. Moreover, Hooligans do not seek for changing the world through revolutionary engagement, which is incompatible with this social movement Model as well. A further stark misperception with regards to explaining Hooliganism is concerning its participants. Neither the members, nor the (in Hooliganism anyway absent) leaders mainly consist of students and young professionals. As a last critique we argue from our normative standpoint that Hooligans are really not the only hope for mankind as the "Cultural Model" calls it sympathetically.

On the positive side, we agree with two points. First, academia has not succeeded in identifying reasons for a declining Hooligan movement which coincides with the "Cultural Model". Secondly, its manifestation as a consensus-based, egalitarian, free phenomenon characterizes very well how Hooligans act in reality. In summary however, the Model discussed here performs poorly in enhancing the understanding of (English) Hooliganism.

The final model under scrutiny, developed amongst others by Scott (1985), and Fox Piven and Cloward (1977), made its way into academia under the name "Defiance Model". Its purpose is mainly to enhance the understanding of rebellions and uprising protests in times of extreme deprivation and repression, such as slavery, mass unemployment, or in ghettos. Even though one can realize right away that none of these general terms fit for the context of English Hooligans, numerous matches can still be observed.

In the beginning, however, the two major misjudgments of that Model shall be looked at. It is argued that a social movement can only occur in the case of major simultaneous social dislocations that finally enable the poor to break the vicious circle of constant repression. England obviously has never been a state of slavery, ghettos or other oppressive instruments during the 20th century. In consequence, a dividing and weakening of the elites was not only unnecessary, but also absent, which disqualifies that explanatory approach for Hooliganism. Also, the notion of a relatively brief duration is mistaken because English Hooligans have been a continuous long-term phenomenon, as we saw when examining their history. For two further categories, we see the hypothesis partly fulfilled with regards to Hooliganism. The participants in the movement in the majority stem from the lower working class, as empirically proven by Dunning (2000). Nonetheless, this does not genuinely correspond to the assumption of the "Defiance Model", which sees the core of a movement in the absolutely lowest class that is basically excluded from society. As we have described that, for example, the ordinary Hooligan is employed and received basic education, and since English Hooliganism also recruits a substantial share of its members from higher social classes, the "Defiance Model" shows an exaggerated depiction. We can also not exactly agree with the way the Model in theory would see the Hooligan movement in operation. On the one hand, resistance is indeed put into practice in an unorganized and anonymous way, and Hooligans attempt to some degree to defy the authorities' regulations. On the other hand, that notion of resistance through defiance puts also heavy emphasis on issues such as abseenteism, strikes, welfare fraud, refusal to vote, sloppy work, or tax evasion. Apart from the fact that data which would indicate for example a tax fraud rate above normal among Hooligans could not be found, such features in general are not what characterizes Hooliganism. English Hooligans actively take part in their movement only on the day of the football game, and do not transfer their behaviour into everyday life outside of the realm of football.

Coming to the consonances, the absence of leaders, as assumed by the "Defiance Model" is exactly what is observable among Hooligans. Furthermore, the two-sided approach for bringing Hooliganism under control (or at least the attempt) is greatly in line with the assumptions of the Model discussed here. There is both professionalization and appeasement through e.g. special fan coaches, and the repression of remaining protesters by the authorities, which took place with the installation of CCTV, increased security staff, etc. Lastly, the recognition in the precedent chapters, that the quite unorganized character of the Hooligan movement makes it very difficult for the elites to tackle it, goes hand in hand with the "Defiance Model" which regards such a form of resistance as effective, too. Yet, the overall impact of the "Defiance" movement is limited and rather small, which is the case for Hooliganism, too.

Summarizing the applicability of the four Models of social movements outlined in this chapter, we conclude with the "Classical" and the "Defiance" Model with the largest share of accordance. The "Political" and the "Cultural" Model are to reject for the explained obvious discrepancies. Pertaining to our two "winning" Models, we are arguing in the last step that the "Classical" Model is to be preferred over the "Defiance" Model for several important reasons. To qualify as a good Model for explaining the English Hooliganism movement, we consider an accurate hypothesis for its rise and growth as pivotal. Having this in mind, the reason for the rise of collective violent behaviour is much better reflected by the "Classical" Model. We are convinced that the rise of the mass society and the modern state are core elements that caused the emergence of the movement. Men feel enslaved by rationality and technology, which results in a loss of identity, personal dislocation and the feeling of a gradual atomization of society. This missing group-belonging, the dissolution of traditional social ties, such as a strong church, lead to irrational thought, hysteria, and the break-out of violence. We recognize Hooligans very well in this hypothesis of the "Classical" Model. The feeling of belonging to a group with a common identity is a way for Hooligans to cope with the vanishing order of how society used to be organized.

A second major argument is that we question, whether Hooligan violence has really a deeper rationale as suggested by the "Defiance" Model. At this point, it is important to come back to the theories of explaining Hooliganism. We agree most with the "reverse psychological" approach, and with Dunning's (2000) hypothesis, which both do not consider Hooliganism as a manifestation of poor people's protests out of suppression. In contrast to the ideas of the "Defiance" Model, we go even one step further. The findings of this paper suggest that Hooligans not only have no deeper rationale in their behaviour, but even want to escape the overly rationalized reality of their everyday life through their actions. Applying to both the lower working-class, but also to white-collar workers, all seek for a break from the ordinary life where emotions are largely repressed and rational bureaucracy dominates. At least during one afternoon of the week, the man can be man again and let his feelings flow uncontrolled within this movement. Moreover, English Hooligans have the need for challenges, for creating "artificial" dangers (Armstrong, 1998, p. 296) and thrilling excitement, as this is absent in their everyday life. Hooligans want to break out and "switch off" their routine life, which also very well explains the excessive amount of alcohol consumed. Why would Hooligans become very drunk, look for risky situations, and try to forget their normal everyday life, if their

14

actions are intended to raise awareness about their oppressed social background? Here, the "Defiance" Model is simply the wrong theory.

As a final remark, also the media attention is sought by Hooligans in order to receive respect, a feeling that is otherwise probably missing. Yet, it is satisfying for them to feel important, and there is not the deeper aim to convey distinct societal intentions through the media.

VI. Deficiencies of the "Classical" Model and adjustments

Until this point, we have advocated the "Classical" Model as the best explanation for the English Hooligan movement. Nevertheless, even in that Model we have not achieved 100% congruence which justifies outlining several adjustment proposals in this part. Especially, as the name already suggests, the Model draws its justification mainly from 'older' movements such as Nazism or Fascism. For updating it for the 21st century, we shall include the role of the media, and also provide a more correct explanation for the duration of such a movement.

Special attention must be devoted to the role of the media for a better understanding of English Hooliganism and social movements in general. Frosdick and Marsh (2005) argue that media play a central role in Hooliganism. They are able to influence and even instigate Hooligan action through two main channels. Media have become known for "predictive" reporting, meaning that a possibly violent clash of two rivalry football fan groups is already heated up in the press in the days prior to the game. Secondly, media have also published informal rankings of English Hooligan "firms" which of course propagates violent and destructive action as each "firm" seeks to be on top and acquire the toughest, most respectable reputation. However, this media interference is in general the case not only for Hooligans. Overall, sensationalist media can trigger violent engagement in social movements and influence the dynamics of collective action. Hence, their role has to be taken into account and thus be included in the social movement Model.

The second adjustment advocated by us is concerned with the duration of the movement. As mentioned before, the 'Classical Model' predicts the movement to be transient whereas Hooligan behaviour, looking at its relatively long history, appears to be a lasting occurrence. This can be explained by the diffusion theory which has been employed to understand the 'spread' of collective behaviour, specifically collective violence (Braun & Vliegenthart, 2008). Thus this approach goes beyond the mere attempt to theorize the emergence of Hooliganism by taking the actual mechanism of how Hooliganism maintains and remains to be relevant into account. Confirming that Hooliganism can indeed be regarded as a social movement and therefore justifying the appliance of the diffusion theory, Braun and Vliegenthart come to their statistically relevant conclusion that Hooligan behaviour *fluctuates* subject to three conditions. First, there is a strong relationship between the likelihood of fan violence and the fact that contentious behaviour was present at the previous game (Ibid., 24). Second, Hooligan behaviour is strongly associated with an increased level of aggressiveness of the football players during the match (Ibid.). This would also support our reasoning that Hooligans seek some sense of belonging in their supporter groups in which they develop a collective identity (Giulianotti & Robertson, 2006). This would make them more susceptible for imitating the behaviour of certain role models (in this case the football players). Finally, there is evidence for fan violence being more 'contagious' between more similar supporters in terms of social status and between clubs that are closer in the league to each other (Braun & Vliegenthart, 2008, p.25). Although these outcomes result from a study conducted in the Netherlands, it is only reasonable to acknowledge them in reference to English Hooliganism suggesting similar research in England. After all, by enhancing diffusion theory when dealing with Hooligan behaviour we do not try to invent a new social movement model so that it would match Hooliganism perfectly. Instead, as diffusion theory is a concept which is applied to social movements in general, the significant association with Hooliganism only enforces the line of argumentation that Hooliganism is a form of collective action. This vindicates the purpose of this paper, namely treating Hooliganism as a social movement that can meaningfully be related to the four most prominent social movement models – considering some adjustments are made.

VII.   Conclusion

In this paper, we aimed at finding out whether Hooliganism can be regarded as a social movement. We looked at its emergence and its enduring occurrence to understand the reasons why people tend to engage in Hooligan action. Juxtaposing the most renowned approaches towards a theoretical understanding of Hooliganism, it could be seen that this violent collective behaviour is mainly rooted in a search for a thrill. It is also perceived that in these Hooligan groups, members find status and meaning by showing off their masculinity. Realizing that it seems exaggerated to see a deeper rationale in their destructive behaviour and rejecting that Hooligans have a higher goal to change their political or societal environment, it was concluded that Hooligans are an untypical social movement. When applying the four Models of social movements, we saw the most consistency with the "Classical Model". Nevertheless, we deemed it necessary to take additional factors into consideration as the "Classical Model" did not deliver sufficient explanations of Hooligans. Reflecting on the media's power to trigger contentious behaviour and the significant outcomes of the appliance of the diffusion theory, we allowed us to make some adjustments for the investigations of Hooliganism.

In the end, it can be stated that Hooliganism may not necessarily need an absolute understanding. As different groups of interest are affected by Hooliganism (the Hooligans, the other 'normal' fans that get disturbed or hurt, the football clubs, the authorities, and the government), there should be different ways to encounter it. The enforcement of the all-seater stadia may have decreased the Hooligan clashes at the actual football grounds, but since the violent actions just moved to other places, it shows that Hooliganism requires other if not more proactive measures. Therefore, in further research it is advisable to look at Hooliganism in a way that considers the interests of all parties involved. Cultural Theory developed by Douglas & Wildavsky (1982) offers this approach which is said to be applicable to most social or political issues. As described by Verweij et al. (2006, p. 836) "Instead of taking sides, Cultural Theory is an effort to outline which combinations of interests, norms, perceptions, time horizons, strategies and emotions prevail in which particular social settings." Not taking sides is maybe exactly what is necessary to encompass the whole phenomenon of Hooliganism. It reveals that the authorities have something different at stake than the Hooligan members and allows for disagreement and conflict of interest. It is just a matter of acknowledging this conflict and by rejecting supreme approaches arriving at one that is purposefully imperfect or "clumsy" as labelled by Verweij et al. (2006, p.839). This approach may help to eventually install a peaceful atmosphere around the most popular sport in the world: Football.

VIII. Bibliography

Armstrong, G. (1998). *Football Hooligans. Knowing The Score*. Oxford, New York: Berg.

Blumer, H. (1969). Collective behavior, in A. McClung-Lee (ed.) *Principles of Sociology*. New York, NY: Barnes and Noble

Boissevain, J. (1974). *Friends of Friends: Networks, Manipulators and Coalitions*. Oxford: Blackwell.

Braun, R. & Vliegenthart, R. (2008-07-31). Violent Fan Fluctuations. Paper presented at the annual meeting of the American Sociological Association Annual Meeting. Sheraton Boston and the Boston Marriott Copley place, Boston, MA Online <PDF>. 2009-03-04 from http://www.allacademic.com/meta/p242440_index.html

Brimson, D. (2000). *The Changing Face of Football Violence*. London: Headline.

Brown, A. (Ed.). (1998). *Fanatics!: power, identity, and fandom in football* . London, New York: Routledge.

Buford, B. (1991). *Geil auf Gewalt. Unter Hooligans*. München, Wien: Carl Hanser Verlag.

Cohen, A. (1974*). Two-Dimensional Man*. An Essay on the Anthropology of Power and Symbolism in Complex Society. London: Routledge and Kegan Paul.

Crossley, N. (2002). *Making sense of social movements*. Buckingham, Philadelphia: Open University Press.

Della Porta, D. and Diani, M. (1999). *Social Movements: An Introduction*. Oxford: Blackwell.

Douglas, M., & Wildavsky, A. (1982). *Risk and Culture: An Essay on the Selection of Technological and Environmental Dangers*. Berkeley, CA: University of California Press.

Durkheim, É. (1893). *De la division du travail social*. Paris: Les Presses universitaires de France.

Durkheim, É. (1897). *Le Suicide*. Paris: Les Presses universitaires de France.

Dunning, E. (2000). Towards a Sociological Understanding of Football Hooliganism as a World Phenomenon. *European Journal on Criminal Policy and Research, 8,* 141–162.

Elias, N., & Dunning, E. (1986). *Quest for Excitement: Sport and Leisure in the Civilizing Process*. Oxford: Blackwell.

Eyerman, R. & Jamison, A. (1991). *Social Movements: A Cognitive Approach*. Cambridge: Polity.

Fox Piven, F., Cloward, R. (1997) *Poor People's Movements: How They Succeed, Why They Fail*. New York: Vintage.

Frosdick, S., & Marsh, P. (2005). *Football Hooliganism*. Cullompton: Willan Publishing.

18

Gardner, P. (1996). *The Simplest Game: The Intelligent Fan's Guide to the World of Soccer.* New York: Maxwell Macmillan International.

Giulianotti, R. (1999) Football: A Sociology of the Global Game. Cambridge: Polity Press.

Giulianotti, R., & Robertson, R. (2006). Glocalization, Globalization and Migration. The Case of Scottish Football Supporters in North America. *International Sociology , 21* (2), 171-198.

Greer, S. (1958). Individual Participation in Mass Society. In R. Yong, *Approaches to the Study of Politics: Twenty-two Contemporary Essays Exploring the Nature of Politics and Methods by Which it Can Be Studied* (pp. 329-342). Evanston, Ill.: Northwestern Univ. Press.

Heberle, R. (1968). Social Movements. In D. S. Sills, *The International Encyclopedia of the Social Sciences* (pp. 438-44). New York: MacMillan.

Home Office. (2008). *Statstics on Football-Related Arrests & Banning Orders Season 2007-08.* London: UK Home Office.

Kerr, J. H. (1994). *Understanding Soccer Hooliganism.* Buckingham, Philadelphia: Open University Press.

Kornhauser, W. (1968) "Mass Society", in D. Sills (ed.) *The International Encyclopaedia of Social Sciences.* New York: MacMillan.

Kriesi, H., Koopmans, R., Duyvendak, J., Giugni, M. (1997) New Social Movements and Political Opportunities in Western Europe; in D. McAdam and D. Snow (eds.) *Social Movements: Readings on Their Emergence, Mobilization and Dynamics.* Los Angeles: Roxbury.

Long, S. (1999) Gay and Lesbian Movements in Eastern Europe: Romania, Hungary, and the Czech Republic in B. Adam, J. Duyvendak, A. Krouwel (eds.) *The Global Emergence of Gay and Lesbian Politics: National Imprints of a Worldwide Movement.* Philadelphia: Temple University Press.

Marcuse, H. (1964) *One-Dimensional Man: Studies in the Ideology of Advanced Industrial Society.* Boston: Beacon Press.

McAdam, D. (1997) Institution-Building in the African American Community, 1931-1954; in D. McAdam and D. Snow (eds.) *Social Movements: Readings on Their Emergence, Mobilization and Dynamics.* Los Angeles: Roxbury.

Parsons, T. (1965). An Outline of the Social System. In T. Parsons, E. Shills, K. D. Naegele, & J. R. Pitts, *Thoeries of Society: Foundations of Modern Sociological Thought.* New York: The Free Press.

Pearson, G. (University of Liverpool FIG Factsheet) www.liv.ac.uk/footballindustry/hooligan.html, accessed May 08, 2009.

Pentz, J. & Köster, P. (n.d.). *Tod am Zaun.* Retrieved May 08, 2009, from http://einestages.spiegel.de/static/topicalbumbackground/3962/tod_am_zaun.html

Scott, J.C. (1985). *Weapons of the Weak: Everyday Forms of Peasants' Resistance.* New Haven, CN: Yale University Press.

Spaaij, R. (2006). *Understanding Football Hooliganism.* Amsterdam: Amsterdam University Press.

Spaaij, R. (2008). Men Like Us, Boys Like Them: Violence, Masculinity, and Collective Identity in Football Hooliganism. *Journal of Sport and Social Issues, 32, 369-392.*

Tarrow, S. (1998). *Power in Movement.* Cambridge: Cambridge University Press.

Taylor, I. (1971). Football mad: A speculative sociology of football hooliganism. In E. Dunning (Ed.), *The Sociology of Sport: A Selection of Readings* (pp. 352-377). London: Frank Cass.

Taylor, I. (1982). Putting the boot into working class sport: British soccer after Bradford and Brussels. *Sociology of Sport Journal , 4,* 171-191.

Tönnies, F. (1957). *Community and Society (Gemeinschaft und Gesellschaft).* East Lansing: Michigan State University Press.

Touraine, A. (1971). *The May Movement: Revolt and Reform; May 1968; the student rebellion and workers' strikes – the birth of a social movement.* New York: Random House.

Verweij, M. et al. (2006). Clumsy Solutions for a Complex World: The Case of Climate Change. *Public Administration , 84* (4), 817-43.

Wagner, H. (2002). *Fußballfans und Hooligans.* Gelnhausen: Wagner.

Williams, J.M., Dunning, E. & Murphy, P. (1984). *Hooligans Abroad.* London, New York: Routledge.

Weber, M. (1946). *From Max Weber: Essays in Sociology. Translated and edited by Hans H. Gerth and C. Writght Mills.* New York: Oxford University Press.

Zimbardo, P. G. (1970). The human choice: Individuation, reason, and order versus deindividuation, impulse, and chaos. In W. J. Arnold, & D. Levine, *1969 Nebraska Symposium on Motivation* (pp. 237-307). Lincoln, NE: University of Nebraska Press.

YOUR KNOWLEDGE HAS VALUE